£1-00

HORSE LAUGHS

The Ups and Downs
of
Three-Day Eventing

Julian Seaman

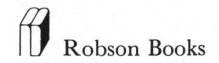

Robson Books

Acknowledgements

Grateful thanks to all the following for their kind permission to include copyright material: Condé Nast for Emmwood's *Tatler* drawings on page 17; Macdonald & Co (Publishers) for the excerpt from *Pigsticking* by Willie Rushton on page 23, and the quotation and drawing from *The Land of England* by Dorothy Hartley on page 59; the *Daily Mail* for the cartoon by Mac on page 28; Pelham Books for the excerpt from *Up, Up and away* by Lucinda Prior-Palmer on page 39; Syndication International for the Keith Waite cartoon on page 45; *Private Eye* for the extracts on page 49; Express Newspapers for the Giles cartoon on page 63; Collins Publishers for the extract from *Paddington Takes the Air* by Michael Bond on page 86; and the editor and proprietors of *Punch* magazine for the David Langdon cartoon on page 88.

Designed by Harold King

FIRST PUBLISHED IN GREAT BRITAIN IN 1983 BY ROBSON BOOKS LTD., BOLSOVER HOUSE, 5-6 CLIPSTONE STREET, LONDON W1P 7EB. COPYRIGHT © 1983 JULIAN SEAMAN

British Library Cataloguing in Publication Data

Seaman, Julian
    Horse laughs.
    1. Three-day event (Horsemanship) – Anecdotes facetiae, satire etc
    I. Title
    798.2′4′0207   SF295.7

ISBN 0-86051-216-9

Printed in Hungary.

Thank you to the following for your hospitality while being "interviewed"

H.R.H. Princess Anne and Captain Mark Phillips
Sue Benson
Duncan McQueen Burns
Tiny Clapham
Chris Collins
Nipper Constance
Mary Gordon-Watson
Lucinda Green
Jane Holderness-Roddam
Lieutenant-Colonel Bill Lithgow
Richard Meade
Lord Hugh Russell and Lady Hugh Russell
Peter Scott-Dunn
Lars Sederholm and Diana Sederholm
Jane Starkey
Dick Stillwell
Hugh Thomas and Ann Thomas
Mike Tucker and Angela Tucker
Richard Walker
Major Malcolm Wallace and Caroline Wallace
Lieutenant-Colonel Frank Weldon
All the Stoneleigh Staff
and all my other friends who have given inspiration – (I hope they still are friends!)

About the author

Once upon a time there was a handsome young sportsman who dreamed of becoming an author. He researched for years to gather information for his project. He was entertained by stars of yesterday, today and tomorrow and finally wrote the most educational, enlightening and readable book that had ever been written about his sport – Golf. Sadly, this book is written by someone else.

Contents

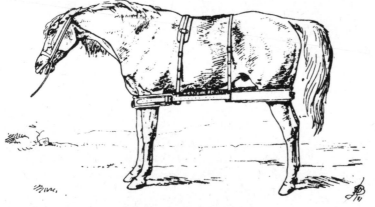

Fig. 54.—Horse with strait-jacket on.

Foreword

by Richard Meade

CHURCH FARM
WEST LITTLETON
CHIPPENHAM
WILTSHIRE SN14 8JB

Dear Julian,

I very much enjoyed reading the draft manuscript.

The book in your flat "Vin Rude" reminded me of the evening in that night club with my Cambridge friends; and the naked dancer who was so ████████ and came so ████ .... and as the champagne ran down how it fizzed when it reached her ████!

We had just come from a Swizzlestick Dinner. Rather appropriate, don't you think!

By the way this is _not_ for publication

Yours ev.,

Richard.

Preface
by Richard Walker

Richard Walker   C/o 3 Priory Bank,

Great Milton,

Oxford.

Dear Julian,

     A preview of your ~~~~~ made for a ~~~~~~~ while indulging in compulsory ~~~~~~~~ with my leg encased in a plaster-cast.

     I was most relieved that you had not recounted the tales about the ~~~~~ after-lunch hang-gliding sortie, the pre-skiing competition for the mirror or ~~~~~~~~~~~~~ (~~~~~~~~~~~) chalet girls

     as ever

       Richard

Introduction
by Lucinda Green

APPLESHAW HOUSE.
ANDOVER.
HAMPSHIRE.
SP11 9BT

WEYHILL 2333
STATION: ANDOVER JUNCTION

Dear Julian —

Delighted for you to ████████ TV

████████ me. Very glad to note that you have not

managed to make some ████████ story out of

a T.V. Appearance on "Game for a Laugh". When

Willy Carson ████████ my backside for what

seemed an eternity —

Good luck. Love Lucinda G

Every picture tells a story

Lambert's Sofa

This is thought to be the earliest photograph of a horse and rider in training for this well-known Burghley obstacle.

See these muscle improvements in 14 days or you pay nothing!

With the revolutionary 'Bum-worker'
1500 gns + carriage

SALES DEPARTMENT, ATLAS HOUSE, FENCING LANE, MIDDLESEX MX3 JSE

Yes, please rush one the revolutionary 'Bum-worker'.

One encloses a cheque/postal order for £1575+£250 carriage

One's groom will collect (*delete whichever is inapplicable*)

Name . . . .

. . . .

. . . .

. . . .

Address . . . .

14

Every picture tells a story

'Down, down to bottomless perdition there to dwell
In adamantine chains and penal fire.'

(*Paradise Lost*, Milton)

'He must be off his trolley'

(The author)

Emmerwood Amongst the three-day event riders

Chris Collins

Mary Gordon-Watson

Mark Phillips

Richard Meade

Princess Anne

Richard Walker

Debbie West

WHO'S WHO

H.R.H. PRINCESS ANNE – A member of the British Olympic Team at Montreal, she has won the European Championship and also been runner-up.

SUE BENSON – A consistent member of the British Team, best remembered for testing the water jump at a foreign event in a bikini.

MICHAEL CLAYTON – Editor of *Horse and Hound*, and is its roving hunting correspondent, Foxford.

CHRIS COLLINS – Former amateur steeplechase champion, a past member of the British 3-Day Event team and currently chairman of the selectors. He used to head the Goya perfume company and now deals in wine.

'NIPPER' CONSTANCE – Formerly senior vet at Badminton.

MARY GORDON-WATSON – Olympic Gold Medallist and former World Champion. Has recently written a book on equitation.

LUCINDA GREEN – Née Prior-Palmer; apart from Richard Meade with his International record, she is the most successful event rider yet with four Badminton wins, two European, and one World Title to her credit. She married Australian International rider David Green in 1981.

DAVID HUNT – Britain's leading professional dressage trainer and rider. Has instructed Mark Phillips, Jane Starkey, Lucinda Green, Sue Benson, Mike and Angela Tucker.

BERTIE HILL – Olympic Gold Medallist (1956), riding H.M. the Queen's horse Countryman. A successful West Country point-to-point rider and one-time British team trainer. Mark Phillips is his most successful former pupil. He now devotes his time to his farm and being a Master of Foxhounds.

JANE HOLDERNESS-RODDAM – As Jane Bullen, she took time off from being a nurse in London to ride at the Mexico Olympics; she has won Badminton twice, and Burghley once.

COLONEL BILL LITHGOW – Former team manager and chairman of the selectors from 1977–80.

RICHARD MEADE – Triple Olympic Gold Medallist, twice Badminton winner, is chairman of a film production company.

CAPTAIN MARK PHILLIPS – Has won Badminton four times to date, equalling the record of Lucinda Green (née Prior-Palmer). Shows no signs of letting up with his Range Rover sponsored horses.

MAJOR LAWRENCE ROOK – Olympic Gold Medallist and Badminton winner, a former chairman of the Horse Trials Group.

LORD HUGH RUSSELL – Chairman of the selectors (1972–76), and with Lady Hugh has for many years been host to the training and departing British teams. They run the popular Wylye three-day event in the Autumn. Disabled Lady Hugh has recently taken up competitive driving. Her mini-moke is a feature of the horse trials scene.

PETER SCOTT-DUNN – For many years has been the senior British team vet.

LARS SEDERHOLM – Swedish trainer based at Waterstock in England; has at some time trained most of the top riders – primarily Richard Walker.

JANE STARKEY – Has represented Britain on several occasions and has typed manuscripts for breeding expert Peter Willet.

DICK STILLWELL – For many years British team trainer. Has instructed Richard Meade, Mary Gordon-Watson, Lucinda Green and more recently Tiny Clapham.

HUGH THOMAS – Member of the British team for the Montreal Olympics, has designed the cross country courses at the Windsor and Rotherfield Park three-day events. Is now employed by British Equestrian Promotions to raise sponsorship for the sport.

RICHARD WALKER – Badminton's youngest winner at 18 in 1969, has since won Burghley twice and is the country's most consistent winner of one-day events.

COLONEL FRANK WELDON – 1956 Olympic Gold Medallist and Badminton winner. Now the autocratic, but very efficient, director and course designer of Badminton.

MARTIN WHITELEY – Chairman of the horse trials group, won Little Badminton twice (run over the same course as a second section). He is a housemaster at Eton.

True Facts

The maximum height for Pony Club jumps is 3ft 6in, only five inches lower than Badminton's maximum of 3ft 11in.

A record penalty mark of 18,130.7 was achieved on the speed and endurance phase at the Berlin games of 1936 by a brave Czechoslovakian rider.

Mary Gordon-Watson can't plait.

A Junior rider, terrified by her ambitious mother's reaction to any mistakes she made, worked out that she got into less trouble for a fall than for an ignominious refusal and perfected a technique of baling out whenever her horse stopped.

It costs between £12,000 and £15,000 to erect the loos for each Badminton.

Henry Wynmalen staged the first public one-day event in Britain on March 29th, 1950.

Burghley and Badminton have confident spectators as well as participants; and some of them are very young. Both occasions make excellent family outings, so that the crowds contain many children; to cope with the inevitable strays the authorities have provided 'pounds' where those found wandering can be taken for retrieval at the end of the day.
   A kind lady spotted a little chap standing on his own and

tentatively suggested she might take him to one as he looked lost, only to be quashed by his reaction. 'Oh no, *mummy's* lost!'

Denmark's Nils Haagensen was 1979 European Champion, despite having evented for only the two previous seasons. But he had represented his country in the dressage at the 1976 Montreal Olympics.

Continental newspapers refer to event girls as a 'Team of Amazons'.

At the time of writing, the main committee of the B.H.S. (including Horse Trials) and Stoneleigh staff includes no fewer than two Generals, thirteen Majors and thirteen Colonels.

Richard Walker takes seven and a half minutes to brush his hair.

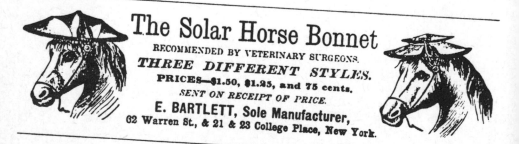

EVENTING ONE'S BILE

The three-day event, as its name suggests, is designed for those who by a quirk of birth, an Act of God, have been blessed with, and view as their due, the long weekend. It is not a reference to Easter, however carefully phrased.

In fact, if you wish to event for Britain, it would be best to pack in any job you have and ride off into the sunset in search of a private income. It is not exactly a sport for all. It's not exactly a spectator sport either, as the cross-country section is extremely difficult to follow, five miles and 35-odd obstacles. Even on television they lose competitors for hours, and unless you get a mild thrill out of watching royalty fall into ponds, not much fun on the course. The first day is boring old dressage, and the third day, on which at least the points system becomes more rational and more easily followed, is Second XI show jumping.

Perhaps you think I'm trying to put you off the whole thing. I would only say this – the horse itself could cost you £5000 for starters, and they're not made of stone, you know, they come apart more easily than humans, particularly in a sport as hairy as eventing. And hairy it be, and you have to take your hat off to those who do it, some of them you are actually obliged to throw yourself bodily out of the way of, bowing and scraping as you go.

RUSHTON: 'Your Royal Highness?

PRINCESS ANNE: 'You bearded twit!'

RUSHTON: 'Would you say Eventing was an elitist pastime?'

PRINCESS ANNE: 'God, you're stupid (cuffs passing child with rolled-up copy of the *Horse and Hound*). Of course it isn't. All one needs is a few acres in the country, paddocks and stabling, the odd groom and a string of horses. Would you mind licking one's boots, one dirtied them on an Expressman? One tells you, it's bloody hard work, and one has other duties to perform, like blanco-ing one's husband. Horses run in the family.'

RUSHTON: 'I know. I always expect your mother at the Trooping of the Colour to suddenly clear three

serried ranks of the 1st Battalion, Coldstream Guards, scatter the orchestra, and set off home across Green Park at pace, hoofing pelicans to death with every stride.'

PRINCESS ANNE: *EXPL*T*V* D*L*T*D*

RUSHTON: 'William Rushton. News at Ten. Badminton.'

PRINCESS ANNE: 'Eventing, you bearded cretin!' (*Fade*)

23

B.H.S. and B.S.J.A NEWS

FROM: The British Equestrian Centre,
Stoneleigh, Kenilworth, Warwicks, CV8 2LR

Tel: Coventry (0203) 52241 (B.H.S.)
Coventry (0203) 552511 (B.S.J.A.)

Have a lesson with Dick Stillwell

This is the age of the trainer

Horses and People

State Opening:

An overheard remark, obviously inspired by the combination of Mark Phillips' royal connections and his controversial sponsorship by ailing British Leyland: 'Things are getting out of hand when one state industry starts sponsoring another.'

Tea-break

Lorna Clarke can manage two cigarettes during the ten-minute halt between phases.

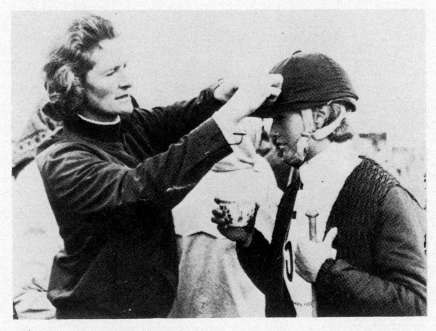

Mary Gordon-Watson had a shot of brandy (discreetly, from a teacup) before going on to win the World Three-Day Eventing Championship in 1970.

Ben Jones used to have a half of bitter.

Lucinda (Prior-Palmer) Green meditates in the loo.

16hh on deck

One of the most remarkable – and successful – feats of preparation was that of the Australian squad in 1960. Horses and riders were loaded on to a slow boat, the deck was covered in sawdust, and animals and humans went into training as they sailed for England and Badminton. The team swept the board at the end of their five-week voyage, and went on to win the team gold at Rome later that year.

Cami Nippers

While it's not unusual for men as well as women to wear tights under their breeches, ex-Badminton vet Nipper Constance went a bit further. He decided that a jock strap was impractical for riding in a team chase, and asked steeplechasing friends for advice. He followed it, but rather wished he hadn't when he fell and was taken to hospital – the nurses, not steeplechasers, were surprised to discover that this horsey man was wearing girls' knickers!

Sam Browne

All the nice girls love a sailor – except those who are attracted to a military uniform. Mary Gordon-Watson remembers feeling more than a little flutter at the sight of Ben Jones competing in his army uniform; and after that her heart skipped a beat when she saw Captain Mark Phillips all dressed up.

Irish Joke

An Irish rider once took the wrong direction in an international event because a leg injury had prevented him from walking the course.

Big For His Boots?

Training with an Olympic squad induces heady nationalist – and other – emotions. Jane Holderness-Roddam was so overcome as she prepared with the team in Mexico for the 1968 Olympics that she quite fell for its Golden Boy, Richard Meade. She came down to earth with a bump, however, when he asked her to clean his boots.

'Hello . . . Captain Mark Phillips seems to be having trouble with one of his new British Leyland-sponsored horses.'

Daily Mail 14th Oct 1979
From the original in the downstairs loo at Gatcombe

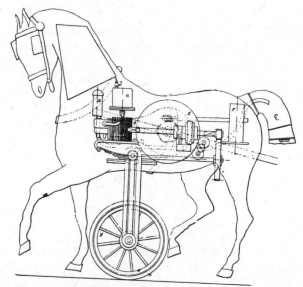

M. Joseph Mille's petrol tractor.

GREAT HORSE BORES
(Apologies to Michael Heath)

"... we bought him as a four-year-old and Amanda worked with him through the winter lots of little indoor shows you know he was 12th in a newcomers and went clear in his first foxhunter and only had two down in the jump-off we were thrilled of course and he's done some little dressage competitions he's not quite between hand and leg yet but he got a 43 last week which is two points better than last time so we're very pleased he's a natural jumper and absolutely pings over his fences Amanda took him to a couple of hunter trials his previous owner had hunted him on a loose rein just the thing he had a few stops but of course he's very young and green but he's got real three-day event potential we are aiming for Badminton 1995 we've entered ten novice trials this season but have been balloted out of eight but of course it's much better not to risk them don't you think it's so nice for Amanda to have another horse because the little mare will be off for another two years, nothing serious but it's stupid to bring them back before they're ready there's just a little bit of heat in the near fore but she's not really a three-day type more of an OI horse but she was the first one we had Amanda brought her up through pony club we're looking for another young one to bring on Amanda has been given a place at a junior trial we haven't got a horse ready yet but of course it will be good experience anyway ..."

29

MAKE YOUR HORSE CUMPHY–

buy him a NAG BAG – you've bought them for your dogs, your children sprawl on them while watching TV. Fully washable luxury for your four-legged friend for only £95.99p –

designs by Zandra Rodeo

Yves St Martin

Christian Eyore

Answers to quiz on pages 90–93

1. b	11. c	21. c
2. b	12. b	22. b
3. c	13. b	23. b
4. a,b and c (and many more)	14. c	24. a
5. b	15. a	25. c
6. b	16. c	26. c
7. c	17. b	27. b
8. a	18. c	28. a
9. a,b and c	19. c	29. c
10. b	20. a	30. b

Score 1 point for each correct answer.

0–5: You watch Badminton or Burghley on the telly if it's raining and there's nothing else to do.

5–10: You make a point of turning the telly on if you think Badminton or Burghley will be on.

10–15: You know people who go to Badminton or Burghley

15–20: You go to Badminton or Burghley as a spectator.

20–25: You go to Badminton or Burghley as a participant.

25–30: Your name was mentioned in this quiz.

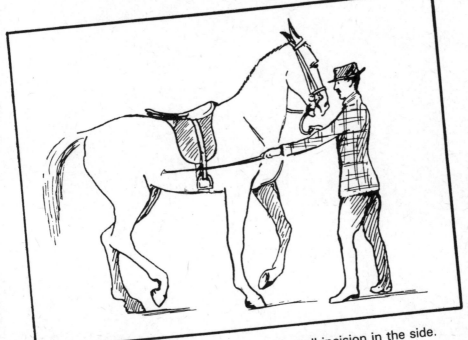

How to remove a tapeworm from a small incision in the side.

Horses and People

Water, Water . . .

In 1951, because of rain, three separate courses had to be built at Badminton before the event could start. Poles were still being put into position on the Friday night before.

. . . Everywhere

There were no public loos at the Rome Olympics of 1960.

A Carriage Horse

Celia Ross-Taylor *and* her horse went to Badminton by train when they first competed.

Like It Or Not

A successful owner expressed a desire to 'get involved in eventing to rub shoulders with the likes of Princess Anne'.

Temper Tantrum

A girl once threw her whip at the inspection panel after her horse had been 'spun' (i.e. failed) in the box at Badminton.

Changing Times

Duncan Mcqueen-Burns of the Midland Bank tells of different attitudes – in 1969 people framed their winner's cheques, or put them in a scrapbook. Nowadays they cash them.

Game of Chance

It's not known whether the powers that be were influenced in their decision to change the marking system for Dressage (giving marks out of 10, rather than out of 6) because speculation was rife that judges' decisions were made by rolling dice.

TOP~TEN FILMS

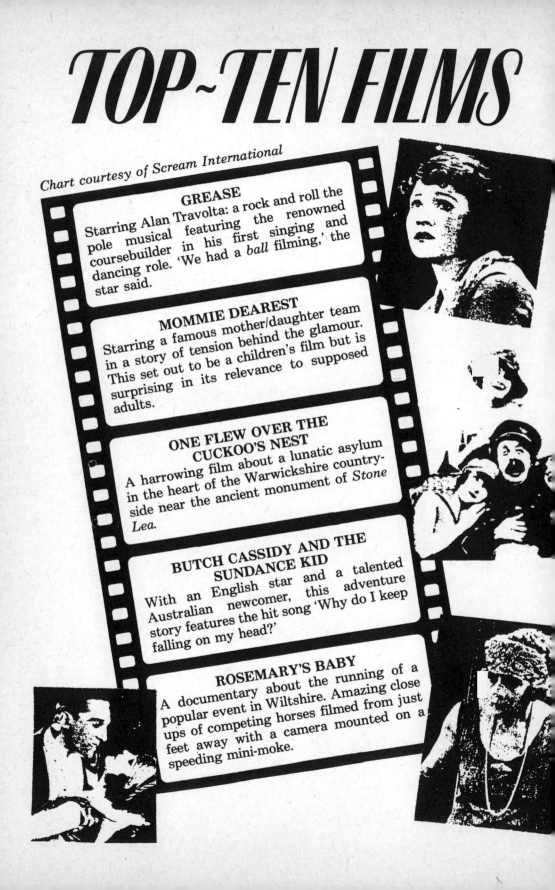

Chart courtesy of Scream International

GREASE
Starring Alan Travolta: a rock and roll the pole musical featuring the renowned coursebuilder in his first singing and dancing role. 'We had a *ball* filming,' the star said.

MOMMIE DEAREST
Starring a famous mother/daughter team in a story of tension behind the glamour. This set out to be a children's film but is surprising in its relevance to supposed adults.

ONE FLEW OVER THE CUCKOO'S NEST
A harrowing film about a lunatic asylum in the heart of the Warwickshire country-side near the ancient monument of *Stone Lea*.

BUTCH CASSIDY AND THE SUNDANCE KID
With an English star and a talented Australian newcomer, this adventure story features the hit song 'Why do I keep falling on my head?'

ROSEMARY'S BABY
A documentary about the running of a popular event in Wiltshire. Amazing close ups of competing horses filmed from just feet away with a camera mounted on a speeding mini-moke.

EASY RIDER
A cult movie about a gang of layabouts driving round the countryside in custom-built trucks, causing havoc wherever they stop. The drug scenes where sachets of bute are passed round are quite horrific.

SATURDAY NIGHT FEVER
This silent film captures brilliantly the manic activity in the horse lines before the final day at Balaclava. Silent music by the Gee Gees.

FANTASIA
This popular cartoon fantasy satirises the belief that the British Film Industry has something to offer its sponsors. Directed by a former Olympic actor, the plot loses momentum early on.

BLAZING SADDLES
A West-country spoof in which 'born again' druids come to the conclusion that riding is a satanic pastime and commit mass suicide in an arson attack on the local tack shop.

THE YOUNG FRANKENSTEIN
A chilling horror movie in which a monster who roams the grounds of a large castle in Weldonia is given the chance once a year to strike terror into the hearts of those who dare attempt his challenge.

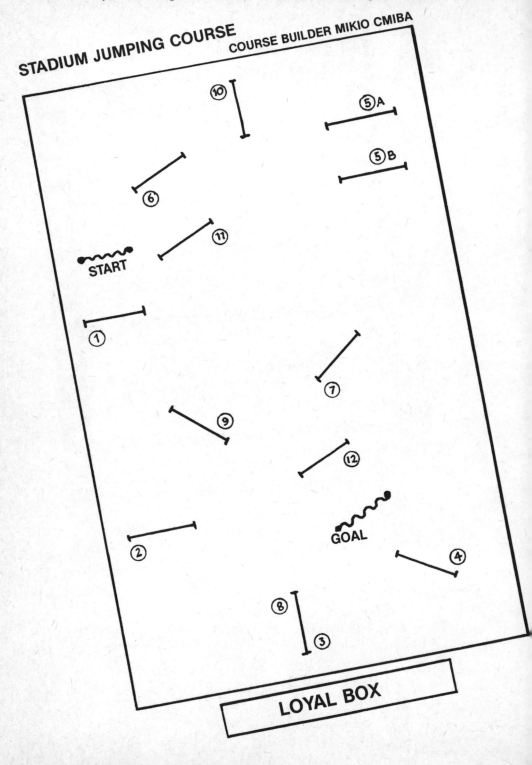

True Facts

The Swiss competition was called 'Gebrauchspferdepru-fungen'.

The number of helpers often equals five times the number of riders at three-day events.

A profit of £20 assured the financial success of the first Badminton in 1949.

'The prevalent notions of the Continental horseman was somebody who spent his time bumming around an arena teasing his horse.' (Col. Hope, *The Horse Trials Story*)

* * * * * * * * * * * * * * * * * * *

A scene from
'Easy Rider'

KITSCH CORNER

Be Fair and I wrote each other letters discussing our thoughts and fancies. Be Fair's spelling of the English language was worse even than my attempts at the French one.

Darling Mum,
I am having a luverlee lazee time in the feeld riggling my bare toez in the graz. Wen r u cuming home agane coz I am longing to start awl owr fun agane.
Lots of luv
Be Fair

I returned to England just in time to fill Be Fair's stocking and creep across the frozen lawn late on Christmas Eve to leave it hanging from the bolt on his door. He had to wait until after church the next day to open it, most of which time he spent trying to nuzzle out of the way the prickly holly stuck in the top, so that he could attack the apples, carrots, polos and sugar lumps which lay wrapped in coloured tissue paper beneath.

Up, Up and Away: Lucinda Prior-Palmer

Jane Holderness-Roddam's horse, Warrior, was overcome by heat exhaustion in the Lexington World Championships of 1978 and failed to complete. The following spring, the pair went into training again and turned up at out-of-the-way hunter trials in remote corners of rural England. Just in case the competition should be too great even under these circumstances, Jane took along Warrior's prettiest rosettes to pin on and bring back his confidence.

Our Special Fancy Ladies' Side Saddle, $7.47.

No. 10K1469 Made on an 18-inch Ruwart tree, fancy pigskin impression skirts stamped on one side, fancy figured seating. Detachable leaping horn, padded and well finished. The bars on this saddle are well padded, so as to be comfortable both for rider and horse. It is made with a 1¼-inch

$7.47

tie strap to tie, with two cinches, soft woven hair. ¾-inch stirrup strap with metal shoe STIRRUP. We would recommend not to buy a cheaper saddle than this one at this exceptionally low price. We guarantee to ship you a saddle better in quality, workmanship and style than can be purchased elsewhere. A careful examination of this saddle will convince you that our description is not exaggerated. Weight of saddle, packed for shipment, about 21 pounds. Price $7.47

Our New Improved Saddle, $11.37.

No. 10K1474 We have found this saddle to be one of the most popular on the market today. It is a good, comfortable, easy riding saddle, well made throughout, no expense having

$11.37

been spared to put in the best workmanship and material. At our exceptionally low price we are sure that it cannot be duplicated elsewhere. The illustrations herewith show both sides of the saddle but in order to appreciate its value it should be carefully inspected. This saddle is made on one of the best quality Ruwart trees with the bars of the saddle padded with sheepskin so as to be easy and comfortable on the horse. Seating is made of fine buckskin with fancy stitching. The SKIRTS on this saddle are 17 inches wide and 15 inches long, made of fine pigskin impression leather, stamped and creased. It has 1¼-inch heavy leather surcingle to buckle and heavy double woven hair CINCHES with iron rings; ¾-inch stirrup strap, with wood leather bottom hooded stirrup. The leaping horns in this saddle are buckskin lined. Heavy under rigging with 1½-inch tie straps on each side. Large, fancy pocket on the off side, which is very handy for carrying papers and any other small articles. If you want a good saddle at a low price we can fully recommend this saddle. Weight of saddle, packed for shipment, about 25 pounds. Price $11.37

Our Indian Prince Stock Saddle, $23.99.

No. 10K1413 This is one of our specially improved heavily built saddles, made on one of the best heavy steel fork trees, raw hide covered. Size of the tree, 15 inches. This tree has been specially improved being made extra strong to stand all kinds of roping. We have used the very best grade of Dundee oak russet saddle

$23.99

skirting and given particular attention to the way the saddle is made and are satisfied that you cannot buy a better saddle at anything like our price. Made with lariat strap on the off side and long lace string on the near side. Solid steel fork tree and horn leather covered. Bound or roll cantle. THE SEAT is well built up, which makes it smooth and easy for the rider. Extra large seamed jockey. Heavy 2½-inch STIRRUP LEATHERS to lace, with a large 16-inch fender attached; steel leather covered STIRRUPS; heavy double rigged saddle; solid over the front and rear, with leather covered steel rings; long 1½-inch TIE STRAPS on the near side to buckle and 1½-inch short ties on the off side to buckle; heavy hair CINCHES with leather chafes and connecting straps, buckle tongues in the cinches, the SKIRTS are sheepskin wool lined, 25 inches long. Remember that this is one of the best bargains in this style of a saddle that you can buy. Popular priced and within the reach of everybody who wants a strictly up to date saddle. Price $23.99

Weight of saddle packed for shipment, about 35 lbs.

Our Light Weight Stock Saddle, $15.27.

No. 10K1429 Made with solid nickel horn is bound or roll cantle. A solid seat and jockey in one piece. THE SEAT is well built up, which makes it very strong. A heavy double rigged saddle with leather covered rings; 1½-inch TIE STRAPS on the near side to buckle and 1½-inch on the off side to buckle; Mexican cotton strings with buckle tongues; Sheepskin wool

$15.27

lined skirts 2 inches long which makes it very easy on the horse. STIRRUP LEATHERS inches wide to lace with 14-inch fender attached and Texas bottom stirrup. Remember that this is one of our popular priced saddles with solid nickel horn, full seat and jockey in one piece. Just the style of saddle that is sure to please those who want a light weight, medium priced stock saddle. Weight of saddle, packed for shipment, about 30 pounds. Price $15.27

Our Fine Chicago Track Bridle.

Made of selected stock, cheeks loop in bit and buckle on crown piece, light overcheck with nose band, light front and rosettes. The finest grade of light driving bridle. Trimmings, nickel or Davis rubber. Weight, about 1½ pounds.

No. 10K1905 Nickel or Davis rubber trimmings. Each.... **$2.30**

No. 10K1909 Genuine rubber trimmings. Price, each.... **$2.53**

If by mail, postage extra, 30 cents.

$2.30

No. 10K1911 Our fine ⅝-inch Flat Cheek Open Bridle, overcheck with nose band, nickel or Davis rubber trimming. Weight, about 1¼ pounds. Price, each. **$1.35** If by mail, postage extra, 29 cents.

$1.35

No. 10K1913 Our fine Open Bridle, ⅝-inch box loop cheeks, layer on crown piece, overcheck with nose band or side rein, fancy front, nickel or Davis rubber trimmings. Weight, about 1½ pounds. Price, each. **$1.57** Postage extra 38c.

$1.57

No. 10K1915 Our Extra Fine Round Open Bridle, overcheck with nose band or round side rein, long layer on crown piece, fancy front. Nickel or Davis rubber trimmings. Weight, about 1½ pounds. Price, each. **$1.73** If by mail, postage extra, 33 cents.

$1.73

No. 10K1922 Our Fine Open Round Rein XC Team Bridle, ⅝-inch scallop cheeks, harness leather front and spotted face piece. Weight, about 2¼ pounds. Price, each **$1.88** Postage, extra, 53c.

No. 10K1923 Same style open bridle as No. 10K1922, only made extra heavy, ⅝-inch open cheek with spotted face piece. Weight, about 2½ pounds. Price, ea. **$2.08** If by mail, postage extra 56 cents.

$1.88

Our $2.38 Team Bridle.

No. 10K1924 Our Fine Round Rein, Long Check, Sensible Blind Team Bridle. Face piece with spots. Extra good team bridle for team work. Weight, 3¼ pounds. Price, ea. **$2.38** If by mail, postage extra, 64 cents.

$2.38

No. 10K1916 This is a good Team Bridle, such as is used on the farm. Made ¾-inch double and stitched cheeks, harness leather sensible blinds, round winker braces, leather front, heavy crown piece, long round rein to check up on the hook on the pad. Weight of bridle, about 3 pounds. Price, each. **$1.89**

No. 10K1917 Same style bridle as No. 10K1916, only made with heavy ⅞-inch cheeks. Price, each. **$2.10** If by mail, postage extra, each 63 cents.

Our Long Cheek Team Bridle.

$1.89

Short Cheek Team Bridle.

$2.00

No. 10K1918 This Bridle is made out of Dundee oak leather, double and stitched ¾-inch cheeks with ring in the end of cheeks, nose band sewed in ring and short bit straps from the ring to the bit, harness leather sensible blinds, round winker braces, heavy front and heavy crown piece, long round rein to check up on the pad. This is a very popular style team bridle. A good, well made bridle. Weight, about 3½ pounds. Price, each. **$2.00**

No. 10K1919 Same style bridle as No. 10K1918, only made with ⅞-inch cheeks. Weight, 3½ pounds. Price, each.................................. **$2.29**

The Course Builders Song

If I had a hammer
I'd hammer in the morning
I'd hammer in the evening
All over this land.
I'd hammer up up-rights
To give you sleepless nights
I'd work out strides between logs, banks and ditches
All over this land.

If I had a digger
I'd digger in the morning
I'd digger in the evening
All over this land.
I'd dig the ditches deeper
Then cover them with creeper
I'd dig holes between the logs and banks and ditches
All over this land.

If I had a chopper
I'd use it in the morning
I'd use it in the evening
All over this land.
I'd build you log piles
I'd build you evil stiles
But leaving stumps between the logs and banks and ditches
All over this land.

Then I'd build a brush fence
I'd stuff it in the morning
I'd stuff it in the evening
All over this land.
I'd stuff it with bendy spruce
To ensure endless use
And relate it to the logs and banks and ditches
All over this land.

(*And so on, and so forth, et cetera*)

42

Every picture tells a story

They arrived late for a schooling session at Wylye.

Colonel Frank Weldon briefs competitors, and reminds them to keep their dogs on the lead in Badminton Park.

Bob Grant of Barraba, jumping 6ft 10in in the pony high jump at Tamworth Show, N.S.W. The most hypercritical of horsemen could not accuse Bob of interfering with his pony's mouth!

Tiny (?!) Clapham

"I've got two more golds, mummy"

Before the 1982 World Championships, Lord Hugh Russell was given these underpants by the British team. The understanding was that if they won the gold medal, he would wear them at the celebration party. With a team and individual success, he sportingly kept his end of the bargain.

Fig. 122.—The mountain zebra.

I did some interesting breaking in of zebras at the Zoological Gardens last March. The first animal I took in hand was Jess, a Grévy zebra mare, which was about nine years old. She stands nearly fifteen hands high and is a very powerful animal. The first problem was how to get a head-stall or halter on Jess in her loose box. A peculiarity about zebras is the extreme sensitiveness of their ears, in which respect they are entirely different from the normal horse. In South Africa and on the Rus-

True Facts

Though smart lady competitors sport a bun beneath their top hats, at least 70 per cent of these buns are detachable.

The earliest report of cross-country jumping instruction is that of the Cavalry of King Charles XI of Sweden as they schooled over cross-country fences in 1688 to the instruction of the riding manual: 'When jumping a fence the rider will grab the mane, close his eyes and shout "hey".'

Although walkie-talkies were confiscated from the Russian team back in the 1960s, at one international competition the behaviour of a Bulgarian competitor in Luhmühlen promoted suspicion that there is more to the Eastern bloc crash-helmets than meets the eye. After one uncomfortable jump the strap of his crash-helmet broke, allowing it to fall to the ground within the penalty zone. Apparently incapable of continuing without it, the luckless competitor returned, dismounted in the zone (thereby incurring 60 penalties) and replaced his hat, whereupon he smiled broadly and continued on his way.

TUESDAY

A MORE gallant officer and gentleman
than Major Charles Vuron Coleville Booth-
Jones never drew breath. He was my
Squadron Leader in the Blues in Cyprus.
Shoulder to shoulder we faced the scream-
ing hordes of Gyppoes, fuzzy-wuzzies and
slant-eyed fanatics demonstrating against
British rule but Charles for one never
flinched.

Now I learn that this same Major has
been beaten up by the Wiltshire police at
Fylye Horse Trials. Three policemen
pinned him to the muddy ground for
fifteen minutes with his wrists handcuffed
and his legs tied together. His crime was to
have suggested a more intelligent way of
organising the traffic.

After two witnesses of good character
had testified that they saw a policeman
approach him from behind and punch him
in the back, he was fined £100 by
Salisbury magistrates for assaulting the
police. The prosecution also claimed he
had said the police inserted a pill into his
mouth in order to dehydrate him, although
he denied saying this.

I would not be in the least surprised.
The Wiltshire police, unlike their
neighbours in Berkshire and Somerset, have
always struck me as utter sods. No doubt
the modern policeman needs these pills
for the war on left-wing schoolteachers,
supporters of Mrs Shirley Williams,
Women against Rape and Lesbians in
Publishing.

But if they start using them against a
lone Major at Horse Trials, we may have
to take the law into our own hands and
travel around everywhere with our own
stock of dehydrating pills and handcuffs.
I for one find the idea most distasteful.

POETRY CORNER

Lines on the Badminton Victory
of June Holderness-Roddam

So.
Congratulations then
June Holderness-Roddam.

You have won.

Lucinda Prior-
Palmer was
Second.

Holderness-Roddam,
Prior-Palmer.

Both
Double-barrelled.

Jarvis-Thribb
Another name
Hyphenated.

But somehow
I do not think
I will ever

Compete
At Badminton.

E. Jarvis-Thribb (17)

Compete at Badminton on

SNAKES AND LADDERS

(formerly ridden by Sheila Willcox)

1 Daddy buys 'nice young horse' +6 *a start*

2 Your mother talks about your horse in the bar for 2 hours to a total stronger −3 *people will be bored with you before they know who you are*

3 Write 12-page letter to Junior Selectors saying how good you are +1 *gives you a boost*

4 'Nice young horse' is slow learner −5 *your're wasting your time*

5 Go on dressage pilgrimage to trainer with foreign name +2 *sounds impressive*

6 Blame yourself not the horse for a disaster −4 *false modesty's useless*

7 Permitted to call Lady Hugh (Russell) 'Rosemary' +20 *you've won Badminton before*

8 You wear earrings while riding in front of Mrs Rook −2 *flashy, though brave*

9 Judges' scores for your dressage show less than 20 discrepancy +4 *amazing*

10 Pay more than £15 for dressage lessons −4 *you're mad*

11 Ride on the 'moke' +6 *you must be arriving*

12 Have a row with Mummy no move *she was probably being as silly as you*

13 Win bursary and refer to Mark Phillips as 'The Captain' +4 *the cash is good*

14 Turn up late for cross-country practice at Wylye −5 *but the repercussions are worse*

15 Leave school with 1 'O'-level +3 *another good start*

50

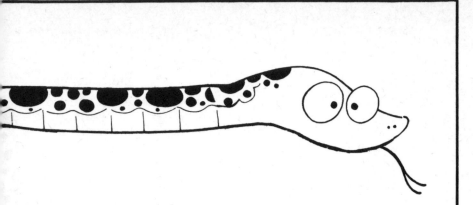

16 Wear Goya scent –1 *good try, but Chris Collins is no longer chairman*

17 Parents offer to be jump judges +5 *some creeping doesn't go amiss*

18 Balloted out of 5 events –4 *your bad luck for being unheard of*

19 Your're described as an amateur +5 *means you don't take yourself* too *seriously*

20 You wear coloured breeches –8 *ugh!*

21 Get a mention in Frank Weldon's Badminton preview –6 *always a bad omen*

22 You discover you have a sense of humour +10 *thank goodness*

23 You write a bleating letter to *Horse & Hound* –2 *just get on with it*

24 Your normal time for getting up is later than 8.00 a.m. +6 *well done, horses like sleep too*

25 You won't go to any party at a 3-day event –7 *you must be very dull*

26 You give your horse Christmas presents no move *it works for some, but luckily not for all*

27 Your bun falls off during the dressage test no move *everyone enjoyed it*

28 You find you have callouses on your hands from mucking out –3 *not feminine, is it, Nigel?*

29 Call Peter Scott-Dunn for your hamster –5 *silly bugger*

Roll dice, and move your sugar cube round the board

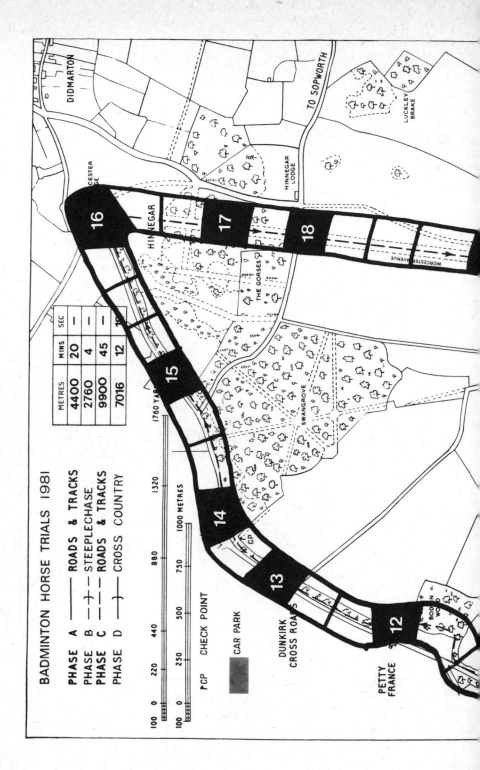

BADMINTON HORSE TRIALS 1981

PHASE A ——— ROADS & TRACKS
PHASE B —+— STEEPLECHASE
PHASE C ——— ROADS & TRACKS
PHASE D —+— CROSS COUNTRY

	METRES	MINS	SEC
	4400	20	—
	2760	4	—
	9900	45	—
	7016	12	15

▶CP CHECK POINT

CAR PARK

DIDMARTON

TO SOPWORTH

LUCKLEY BRAKE

HINNEGAR LODGE

CESTER GE

HINNEGAR

THE GORSES

WORCESTER AVENUE

SWANGROVE

DUNKIRK CROSS ROADS

PETTY FRANCE

BODIN WO

CP

1760 YARDS

1320

880 750

500 440

250 220

100 0

1000 METRES

100 0

12 13 14 15 16 17 18

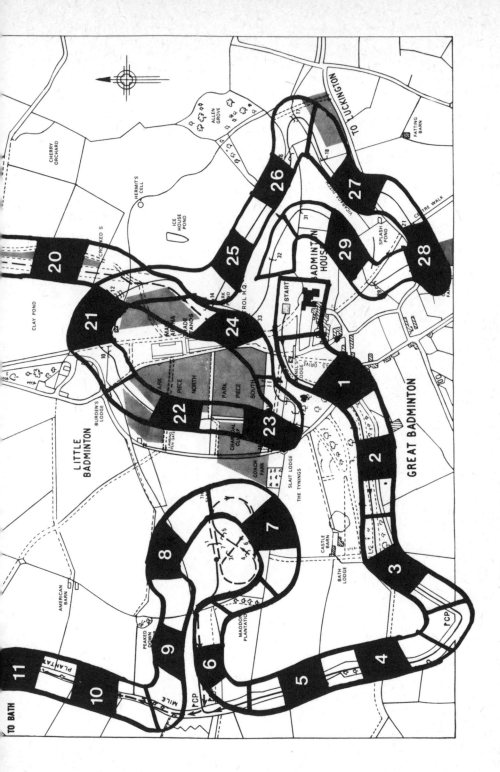

Who Dares Wins

Members of the crack B.H.S. regiment whose exploits abroad are seldom reported by the national press for obvious reasons.

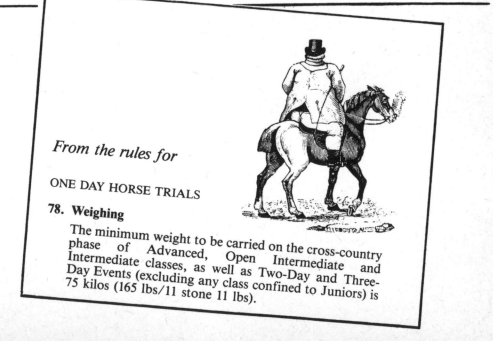
From the rules for

ONE DAY HORSE TRIALS

78. Weighing

The minimum weight to be carried on the cross-country phase of Advanced, Open Intermediate and Intermediate classes, as well as Two-Day and Three-Day Events (excluding any class confined to Juniors) is 75 kilos (165 lbs/11 stone 11 lbs).

Points of the Eventer

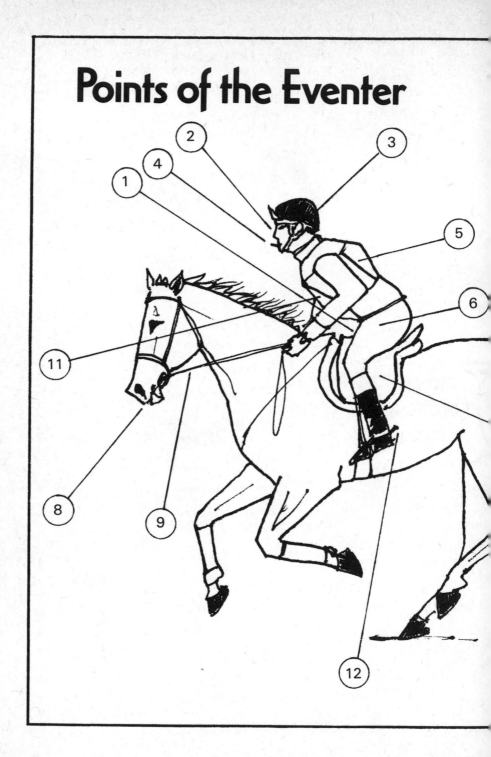

1   gold spare safety pin for flies by ASSPERYS

2   aftershave by BUTE (''splash it all over'')

3   personal stereo 'Canterman' by FIRRIPS (no relation)

4   cigarettes by DUNGHILL

5   number cloth by HUNTLEY & PALMER

6   tights by QUAINT

7   saddle upholstery by CHARLES HAMMOND

8   bridle by HERPES OF PARIS

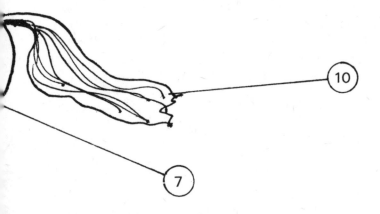

9   reins by RAYNES

10   mane and tail by roger at BRIDLE SASSOON

11   sweater by FRIESIANS GALORE

12   spurs by AND SO TO BED

True Facts

A problem at Badminton is that most of the course, whose construction by the Willis Brothers starts in the previous September, has to be almost totally dismantled every year by direction of the Duke of Beaufort, who prefers his park to look as it did 300 years ago.

One year at Tidworth, Director Major Tony Wootton told riders to try and ignore the obscene graffiti daubed on a jump by local yobos.

Early show jumping penalties were as follows:
1 point for touching show-jump, 2 for hind legs, 4 for fore legs

The French can probably claim to have staged the first recognisable three-day event. In 1902 the Championnat du Cheval d'Armes was staged, for officers only. The obligatory dressage test, which was ridden on the first day, was a fairly simple one, but extra points could be gained in the optional reprise libre or freestyle. Some took this more seriously than others; suffice it is to say that the overall winner of this stage offered shoulder in, serpentines, canter on two tracks, half turns on haunches and forehand without changing pace or gait, changing the leg in four-time, two-time and at every stride. He also performed a piaffe on the spot and backwards, the Spanish walk forward and backwards and on the spot and finally a backwards canter.

In the first Badminton schedule riders were told that accommodation would be organised for competitors' grooms and chauffeurs!

Frank Weldon claims to have invented the 'bounce'.

International Velvet was a box office failure in Britain, but did very well in Mombasa.

One official was given the job of washing four and a half miles of white tape before Burghley!

Crowds in Kiev, Russia, were brought in from local factories to watch the European championships.

* * * * * * * * * * * * * * *

Their bridles are not very brave,
their saddles are but plaine.
             On Russia, George Turberville (1540?–1610?)

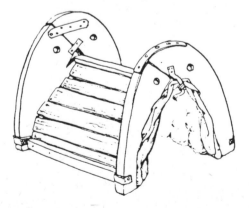

WHAT IS DRESSAGE?

Camp David Talks

As explained in simple terms

Yes well, it's all about *impulsion*, and of course *engagement* of the *hocks*, they want to be *going forward*, but with *elevation*, showing *elasticity* and *suppleness*, they must always be *between hand and leg* and *on the bridle* and before extending it's useful to *collect them* a bit. In *lateral work* the *quarters* mustn't lead. Sometimes they have a tendency to *overbend* which can be the result of not *coming through* but this can also lead to them becoming well *above the vertical* and *resisting the aids*. Probably the most difficult movement in the event test is the *half-pass* though *striking off* up the centre line presents its problems. One must be careful not to *change legs* when performing the *serpentine* since *flying changes* are not required at this level.

One is slightly restricted in the tack to use. No *martingale*, nothing other than a *simple snaffle* or *plain double*, though a *grackle* is permitted. A *numnah* is optional.

If this makes sense I'm a Corsican

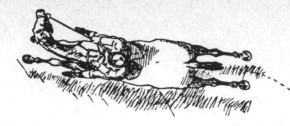
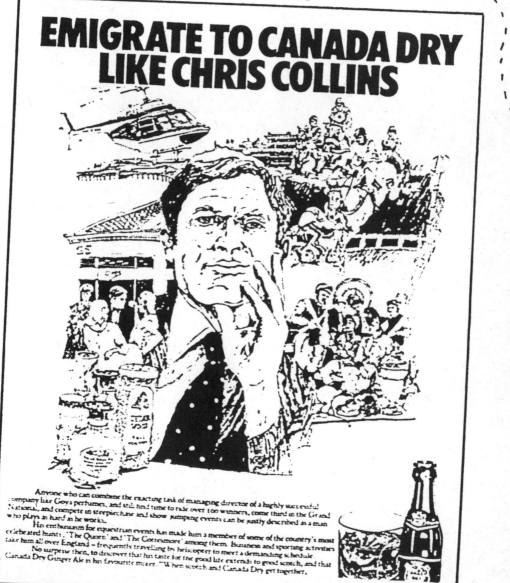

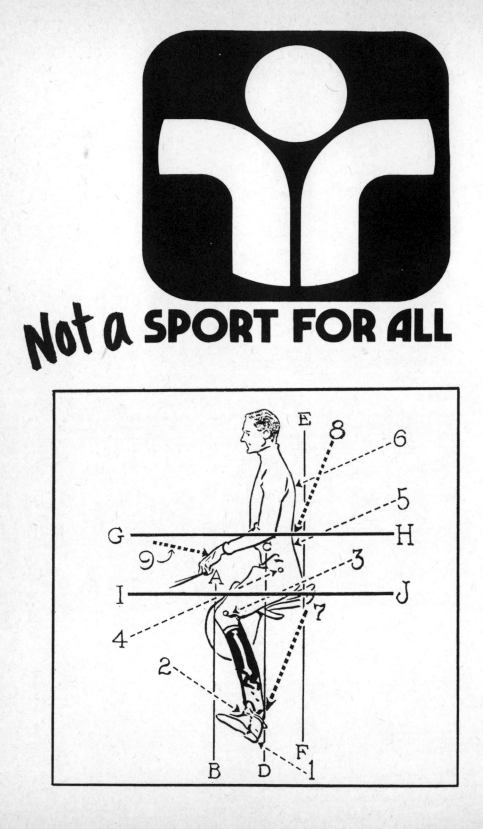

Not a SPORT FOR ALL

Every picture tells a story

You can't take a white horse *any*where!

"Lady, you don't happen to have one about horses being unfair to riders?"

Every picture tells a story

GENERAL ALEXANDER RODZIANKO JUMPING A HAYCART

A MEMBER OF CAPTAIN ANSELL'S TRICK RIDE JUMPING A SWORD

The team and individuals which will be representing Great Britain at next week's world championships

Fig. 104.—Buckjumping saddle.

✳ Two-way competition ✳

● **Spot the rider**   ● **Spot the jump**

Put a cross where you think the centre of either rider or
jump should be. The first correct entry opened will win a

LORST and FOUND

I freely admit that I'm now totally skint because of horses – White Coats

The Feed of Champions

FILLERS | **FILLERS** | **FILLERS** | **KILLERS**

FILLERS
HORSE CUBES

Dear Sir

I feel I must draw your readers' attention to the continuing debate . . . waffle waffle waffle waffle waffle . . . bute waffle waffle waffle waffle . . ., and therefore I must warn against it.
Anna Bollick-Steroid
Little Dormit
Surrey

Dear Sir

I was very interested to read in an October issue . . . waffle waffle waffle waffle waffle waffle hunting dress waffle waffle waffle . . ., so perhaps other elderly subscribers would care to contact me?
D. Nerve
Shavings
Isle of Bute

Dear Sir

Those of us who care deeply for animals (even the two-legged non-feathered variety!) . . . show judges waffle waffle waffle waffle waffle waffle waffle waffle . . .
and then they'll really show the judges!
Annie Seed
League against everything
Hampstead

Dear Sir

I drive to the Continent at least twice a month . . . waffle waffle waffle waffle waffle . . . tachographs waffle waffle waffle waffle . . . or there might be an accident.
Boo Somes
Feltham
Alover
Andover, Andover
Again
Hants

Dear Sir

When one who has been bringing on young horses for almost 50 years . . . waffle waffle waffle waffle waffle balancing rain waffle waffle waffle waffle waffle waffle waffle waffle . . . but lunging is still what I would advise.
Desmond Girth-Gall (Miss)
Lurcher Cottage
Dung Hill
Glos

Dear Sir

Fancy foreign habits are becoming more and more prevalent . . . waffle waffle waffle waffle waffle . . . interval training waffle waffle . . . which would undoubtedly give us better horses.
Colin Bogie MRCVS
Bog Spavin
Chain
Lincs

Dear Sir

Readers with long memories . . . waffle waffle waffle waffle waffle waffle served the hunt for 103 years waffle . . . waffle waffle waffle waffle waffle it seems that side-saddles did have advantages.
Sue Barrew
4, Wheel-Drive Estate
Wembley

Dear Sir

An idea I have used with some success . . . waffle waffle waffle waffle waffle waffle . . . blowing up horse's noses when jumping . . . waffle waffle waffle waffle . . ., and even cattle!
Barbara Logg-Cabin
Walkies
Crufts
Warks

PRINCIPAL CONTENTS

Offices – Overreach Tower, Stamford Street, London SE1
Advertising – Lavatory House, Lavatory Street, London SE1

Badminton.   1949.

No	HORSE	PENALTY POINTS			GRAND TOTAL	PLACE
		1st day	2nd day	3rd day		
1	Guinea Fowl	191	2	withdrawn		
3	Nuthatch	14 137	73	20	250	9th
4	Fourth Hussar	134	Eliminated			
6	Golden Archer	91	Eliminated			
7	Fritzy	89 125	73	10	208	8th
9	Remus	1 56	61	34½	151½	6th
11	Minster Green	17 146	-18	40	168	7th
13	April	16 142	Eliminated			
15	Dandy Dick	233	325	20	578	13th
16	Neptune	172	-54	10	128	5th
19	Varne	6 104	390	43	537	12th
22	Freddie	178½	Eliminated			
26	Proud Robert	130	Eliminated			
29	Golden Willow	90	-63	10	37	1st
31	Cool Star	114½	160	10	284½	10th
33	Black Boy	14 137	Eliminated			
35	Salome	167	16	Eliminated		
38	Stealaway	130	146	13½	289½	11th
40	Titus III	95½	-22	32	105½	3rd
41	Steadfast III	13 136	Eliminated			
43	Sea Lark	114½	-51	—	63½	2nd
44	Lucky Chance	89	-4	34½	119½	4th

The original score sheet of the first Badminton, written by the scorer, Jane Pontifex.

Fences at Badminton 1995

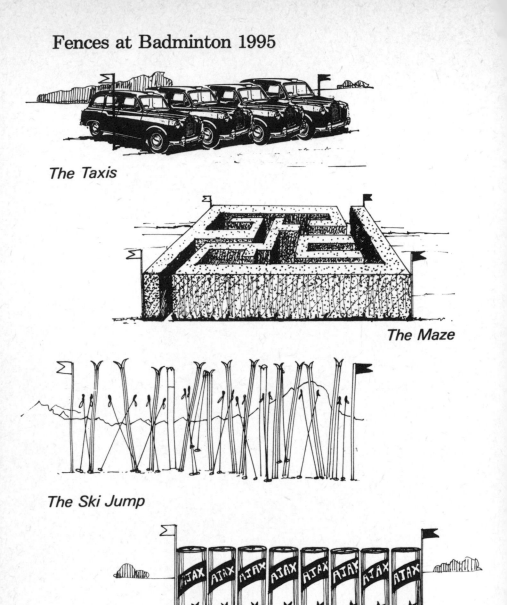

The Taxis

The Maze

The Ski Jump

"Bleachers"

The Timber Wagon

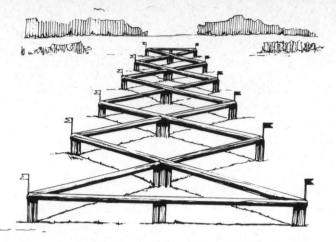

The Chris-Cross

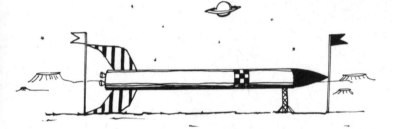

The Into Space

The Double Oxer

The Table

Horses and People

Name of the Game

A few names to show how open to all is the sport of eventing: Fox-Pitt, Connolly-Carrew, Hely-Hutchinson, Martin-Bird, Fleming-Williams, Naylor-Leyland, Ross-Taylor, Cabel-Manners, Machin-Goodall, Wickham-Musgrave, Gordon-Watson, Graham-Young, Lawson-Baker, Dobson-Seaton, Thomson-Jones, Wright-Gibbins, Marsh-Smith, Spencer-Cox, (Brooks-Ward) Prior-Palmer-Green . . . Ad-Nauseam.

Feminine Wiles

Part of the Dressage kit for the girls is vivid lipstick and make-up. To impress the male judges.

From Russia With ...

During the 1968 Mexico Olympics, veteran Australian competitor Bill Roycroft was riding peacefully on phase C when a burly man with a suspiciously short haircut and a voluminous overcoat leaped from behind a bush and lunged at the horse's shoulder with a syringe. Roycroft's cries of protestation only just prevented any contact.

Later, thinking over this bizarre event, he realised that he had overtaken a Russian competitor on phase B – obviously the man with the magic injection had mistaken his target.

Front Loader

Travelling is never without incident. Lochinvar (Derek Allhusen's Silver Medallist ride in the Mexico Olympics) was being loaded into the stalls, which are later hoisted into the aeroplane, on the tarmac before flying to an international event. One of the travel agent's helpers smacked him on the head, thinking to make him lower it to fit under the cross-bar. Instead, Lochinvar shot backwards, slipped out of his bridle and scampered across the vast open spaces of the world's second busiest airport.

Clever Clogs

Richard Meade showed more than entente cordiale one year at Boekelo when he wore a pair of clogs to trot up his horse before the inspection committee on the final day. Only those who had got up bright and early noticed that the horse was, in fact, a little stiff!

Kentucky Fried Chicken

Talking about the disaster caused by the heat in the Lexington World Championships of 1978, one high-ranking British official was heard to comment: 'They shouldn't have expected us to bat on such a sticky wicket,' but 'It was my fault. The problem was, my boy, that I was brought up in India and just didn't realise how hot it was.'

One of the Old School

After a heavy fall at the Helsinki Olympics of 1952, Lawrence Rook had cold water poured over his head, was remounted and pointed in the right direction. He finished the course in a state of semi-consciousness; but, sadly, missed the finishing flags.

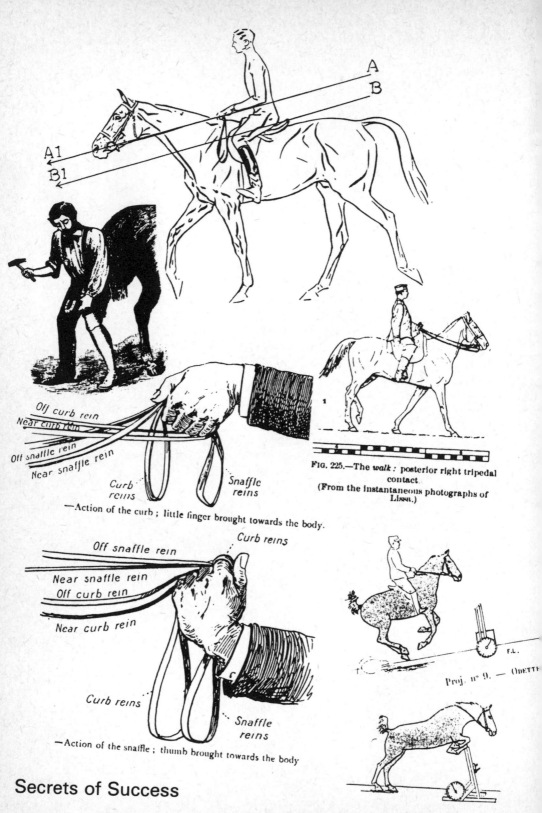

Off curb rein
Near curb rein
Off snaffle rein
Near snaffle rein

Curb
reins

Snaffle
reins

—Action of the curb ; little finger brought towards the body.

FIG. 225.—The *walk* : posterior right tripedal contact.
(From the instantaneous photographs of Lieen.)

Off snaffle rein
Curb reins
Near snaffle rein
Off curb rein
Near curb rein

Curb reins

Snaffle
reins

—Action of the snaffle ; thumb brought towards the body.

Proj. n° 9. — ODETTE

Proj. n° 11.

Secrets of Success

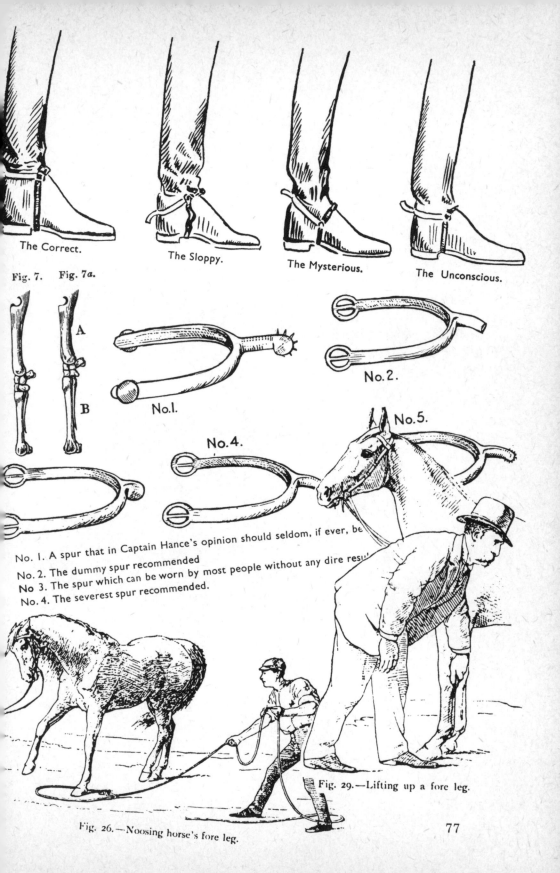

The Correct.

The Sloppy.

The Mysterious.

The Unconscious.

Fig. 7.   Fig. 7a.

A

B

No. 1.

No. 2.

No. 4.

No. 5.

No. 1. A spur that in Captain Hance's opinion should seldom, if ever, be

No. 2. The dummy spur recommended

No. 3. The spur which can be worn by most people without any dire res

No. 4. The severest spur recommended.

Fig. 29.—Lifting up a fore leg.

Fig. 26.—Noosing horse's fore leg.

Eulogy to the Colonels

Where in this wide world can man find
Pomposity without parallel, blimps without exception
And Scotch without water?

Here – where the buck is passed with grace, and committees
To gentlemen confined.

They've done their bit in their time.
They fought in the Boer War.
There is nothing so pleasant.
Nothing very demanding in a retirement job at
The BHS. England's past has been their responsibility.
Go on, give them a break . . .

Near fore, Cornishman

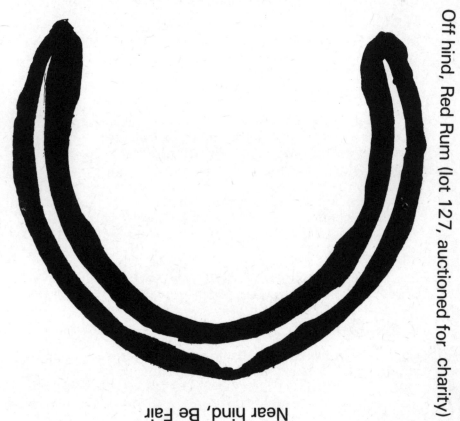

Near hind, The Poacher

Off hind, Red Rum (lot 127, auctioned for charity)

Near hind, Be Fair

Horses and People

Watership Down

At dinner one night, Bruce Davidson of the USA was extolling the virtues of minute-accurate interval training as practised by his squad. He asked Debbie West, our Silver Medallist to Princess Anne's European Championship, how the British got their horses fit.

Debbie winked at the other British riders and, with a straight face, told Bruce that she was very lucky – she had a wood nearby with ruts, holes and deep mud. All she had to do was to gallop her horses up and down this for twenty minutes a day, and they'd soon be fit as a fiddle.

Caroline Silver's book *Eventing* gives the impression that Bruce took her seriously: 'Bruce Davidson was amazed at the casual training methods of the British: how can you expect to get a horse fit in a wood full of rabbit holes?'

Catch Phase

Jane Holderness-Roddam caught Our Nobby's tail, having tripped while running alongside him on the Roads and Tracks in the Mexico Olympics.

Take Me To Your Leader

Malcolm Wallace had no trouble taking his team out to Germany for the European Championships in 1978 but had a little more difficulty coming back. He had enlisted the trusty services of Reggie Purbrick, husband of Lizzie (nee Boone) who rode Felday Farmer round the cross country with no stirrups; (one broke early on so she tossed the other away!) Reggie was second in command of the 17th/21st Queen's Royal Lancers (who had been stationed near Lümuhlen for several years) so his knowledge of the route to the England-bound ferries at Hamburg was second to none. It was arranged that the convoy of British horse boxes should follow Reggie's grey Mercedes while Malcolm drove behind to pick up any stragglers. His job was an easy one because nobody broke down. However, he soon became alarmed when, reckoning Hamburg still to be over forty kilometres away, his convoy led him off the autobahn and down some very narrow country lanes. In no position to question the route, he was helpless to do anything but follow. Meanwhile up ahead, the grey Mercedes turned off the country lanes, down a cobbled road and finally, indicating right, turned into a farm drive. The astounded driver of the front horse box felt quite unable to follow and anyway had been anxious for some time that things were not altogether quite right. Their suspicions were confirmed when the driver of the Mercedes jumped out and embraced warmly the frau who had come running from the farmhouse. There is more than one grey Mercedes car in Germany!

The Price of Fame

Lucinda (Prior-Palmer) Green thought she had scored a hit with the footballer Emlyn Hughes when they appeared together on a TV show for which he was a regular panellist. She watched it the following week – and was mortified when her photograph was used for a question. Hughes not only didn't recognise her, he couldn't even remember her.

HOW TO BE A REALLY SMOOTH WALKER

Hair or Bare?
If you're happy to go with the natural look of hair on your legs, that's fine. But most women still choose to remove the hair on their legs un... very fair and ... If you have a ... hair growth, i... possible to ac... this downy loo... using a mild ... bleaching proc... If your leg hair... too thick for this... treatment, and y... want to remove... there are three... ways to do so, ea... with its own advantages and disadvantages. These methods are shaving, depilatory creams, lotions and foams and waxing.

A Close Shave
Shaving is the cheapest and most popular method of hair-removal. Althou... ... ... good buy. Use it on absolutely dry legs —before not after you bathe.
Be generous with body lotion—as shaving does remove the natural body oils.

Nice and Creamy?
Depilatory creams, lotions and foams are used by... ... ...these products, so always do a patch, test before using a new brand.
We found creams and lotions less messy than the foam which seems to go everywhere.

Wax Away
Waxing is the most effective way to remove hair, but can be painful. It's best to have your first waxing session at a salon where the operator will remove the strips faster than you can say "ouch" and slap the skin to reduce the tingling. A professional wax is worthwhile before ...holiday as it takes up to 4 weeks for the ...ir to grow back. ...you're brave, ...vest in a home hot-waxing kit. These kits will keep you smooth but are no good for the faint-hearted.

GREAT HORSE BORES

". . . of course I don't believe in using bute I mean no one really knows the damage it does and if the horses aren't sound it negates the whole point of the competition anyway and in the long run of course it would be much better for the sport if it were banned now although it would take away many of the top horses but it would give some others a chance how can they hope to break into the big time when so many old horses are being kept going by drugs which negates the whole point of the competition but there's always the chance of course that other undetectable drugs would then be developed or the unscrupulous would denerve their horses from the neck down but of course if people were going to go to those lengths they would be negating the whole point of the sport I mean it's getting so professional now I blame it all on sponsorship I mean no one has got the right attitude today of course if I was in line for a gold medal and the horse had just knocked himself but I knew it wasn't serious but you can hardly explain that to the ground jury I'd probably give him a couple of packets but of course that's different isn't it I mean after all those years waiting for this moment all the training and expense well I would probably use bute then but I'd never use one of those balancing rein jobs for schooling – I mean no-one really knows the damage they can do . . ."

Adrian Ffooks and the author, testing the lake at Badminton in order to decide whether to fall there in the afternoon.

Was this rider testing the quality of the free 'snorts' provided after the Dressage phase?

Every picture tells a story

Steel pier diving horse, Atlantic City. The horse was sent up to a diving board, which was then collapsed under it so that the horse dived into the pool. A daily show.

Clearing 8ft 3½in: Mr Fred Wettach, Junr., on King's Own, an Irish-bred jumper, setting what was believed to be an unofficial world record in the USA in 1928. (To be recognised, a record must be made under official auspices at a public show, where the bars must not be in any way fixed.)

Gay Cheeseman, the famous Olympic rider, had very kindly agreed to judge the contests and act as commentator, and with the sun shining down from a cloudless sky, the sound of horses' hooves pounding the turf, the murmur of the large crowd which had gathered round the sports field, and the creaking of innumerable picnic baskets, it promised to be a memorable occasion.

The roar of excitement as Paddington mounted his horse was equalled only by the groan of disappointment which went up as he disappeared from view over the other side. And when he eventually reappeared facing the wrong way an ominous silence fell over the field; a silence broken only by the crash of falling fences and a cry of rage from Mr. Cheeseman as he watched his best hat being ground to pulp.

Paddington was more upset than anyone.

The Gee Gees –
Saturday Night Fever

Available on A&M Records and Tapes

"Oddly enough their R.S.P.C.A. objects, but not their Royal Humane Society."

By Barty Glenn
& Stuart Harris

FOCUS ON FACT— The Llewellyns

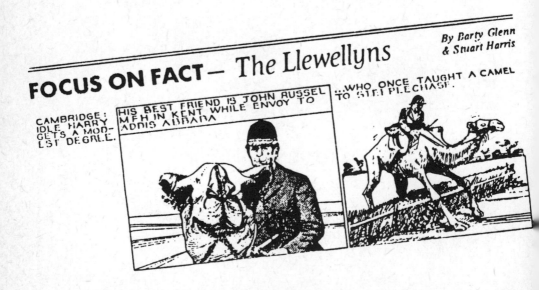

CAMBRIDGE: IDLE HARRY GETS A MODEST DEGREE.

HIS BEST FRIEND IS JOHN RUSSEL MFH IN KENT WHILE ENVOY TO ADDIS ABABA

WHO ONCE TAUGHT A CAMEL TO STEEPLECHASE.

A GOSSIPS QUIZ
with answers

1. **Jean Rook is:**
a) Mrs Lawrence Rook
b) A journalist
c) A chess move

2. **Badminton director Colonel Frank Weldon's last admitted mistake was in:**
a) 1973
b) 1935
c) 1980

3. **Chairman of the selectors Chris Collins highest Grand National placing was:**
a) 5th
b) 7th
c) 3rd

4. **Olympic superstar Richard Meade is known as:**
a) Lord Meade
b) Golden Boy
c) Himself

5. **Angela Meade is known as:**
a) Fiddles
b) Tiddles
c) Piddles

6. **Which trainer often accuses his pupils of riding like 'Cowboys and bloody Indians'?**
a) Bertie Hill
b) Dick Stillwell
c) David Hunt

7. **British team vet, well-built Peter Scott-Dunn's favourite between-meals nibble is:**
a) Twix
b) Lion Bar
c) Mars Bar

8. **Cross-country commentators at Wylye are reminded that:**
a) There are no hills at Wylye
b) Don't talk with your mouth full
c) Drinks are on the house

9. **Which rider doubled for Tatum O'Neal in the eventing feature film, *International Velvet*?**
a) Jane Holderness-Roddam
b) Ginny Holgate
c) Peter Pockock

10. Which top event horse starred in the Dick Francis film,
Dead Cert?
a) The Poacher
b) Cornishman V
c) Cornishman

11. Who said, 'Girls are better with young horses. They
appeal to their mothering instincts?'
a) Richard Pitman
b) Richard Walker
c) Richard Meade

12. Which commentator was once riding at Burghley, but
went to London for a night out with some German riders?
a) Hugh Thomas
b) Mike Tucker
c) Malcolm Wallace

13. Three chefs d'equipes, Major Malcolm Wallace, Colonel
Frank Weldon and Colonel Bill Lithgow, have something in
common:
a) Eton
b) The Kings Troop
c) A Daihatsu

14. Caroline Wallace once worked for:
a) Richard Meade
b) Mark Phillips
c) Princess Anne

15. Horse trials chairman Martin Whiteley is known as:
a) The Schoolmaster
b) Kermit
c) The Godfather

16. Who modelled leather at a fashion show?
a) Richard Walker
b) Ginny Holgate
c) David Hunt

17. Lorna Clarke's famous horse was called:
a) Chili Con Carne
b) Poppadom
c) Pepperpot

18. Which horse fell at the last fence at Badminton, and the
penultimate at Burghley?
a) Rough and Tough
b) Demi Douzaine
c) George

19. Who was fooled into chatting up a subaltern in drag at the Tidworth Ball:
a) Mark Phillips
b) Chris Collins
c) Richard Meade

20. Who call themselves 'Grubbies':
a) Top horse trials grooms
b) Badminton estate workers
c) Stoneleigh staff

21. Who was called to a disciplinary meeting for falling four times at Badminton and continuing, said 'I'll plead concussion,' but was suspended nevertheless:
a) Matthew Straker
b) The author
c) Ernie Fenwick

22. Which top event horse was 'illegitimate'?
a) Carawich
b) Be Fair
c) Great Ovation

23. Princess Anne has said that, had things been different, she would like to have been:
a) A trapeze artist
b) A truck driver
c) A nurse

24. Galloping nurse Jane Holderness-Roddam hurt her back by:
a) Being crushed by dieting 24-stone hospital patient
b) Falling at the Mexico Olympics
c) Hang gliding

25. Which Irish international rider was once called Norman Waters:
a) Gerry Sinnot
b) Jessica Harrington
c) Van de Vater

26. Irish chef d'equipe Jock Ferrie was once a:
a) Weight lifter
b) Boxer
c) Top dressage rider

27. Returning from Boekelo on the ferry, Princess Anne noticed a reminder of the celebration party the year before. It was:
a) A broken table
b) A butter pat on the ceiling
c) The same Captain

28. Grooming for Richard Meade and Cornishman V at the Mexico Olympics was:
a) Mike Tucker
b) Jane Starkey
c) Mary Gordon-Watson

29. At which international event is the winning team awarded a 3ft long cake?
a) Luhmühlen
b) Puncheston
c) Boekelo

30. Interval training is:
a) A form of contraception
b) An American craze
c) Learning how to buy a drink at the theatre

Answers on page 31

" SHE'S LUCKY REALLY, HAD THIS HAPPENED THREE WEEKS AGO IT WOULD PROBABLY HAVE KILLED HER".

True Facts

The World Championships at Lexington in 1978 had an all-time record of over 800 listed officials and helpers.

Sue Benson passed English Literature and Art 'A' levels, but failed Religious Knowledge.

The first Midland Bank sponsored event was Crookham at Tweseldown, Hants in 1969.

Eight of the 22 starters failed to get past the cross-country phase at the first Badminton, including the valiant Brigadier J. Scott-Coburn who was 'three times winner of the Kadir Cup, the pig sticking blue riband of India'.

Horse Trial competitions, according to General Tupper Cole, were regarded by the US Army as 'a military event based on the duty of the officer courier who got through or died'.

At Burghley, parking receipts were suspiciously low one year – despite what appeared to be normal crowds. The organisers were able to check the discrepancy by referring to an aerial photo of the event they had commissioned, and counting the cars. The parking contractors were replaced.

The French have referred to eventing as 'L'épreuve au fond'.

At an Irish event one year the starter for phase D had gone fishing. The event was delayed till he could be found.

Three quarters of the coaches at Badminton are hired by ponyclub and riding club parties. Until it was turned into a more compact figure of eight, the steeplechase course at Badminton had a kink in it – to accommodate even more coaches.

Televising championships causes problems. A course designer, whose fences provided riders with exactly the right combination of challenge and achievement, was given his instructions for the next time: 'Make the water jump more difficult. We want some splashes. Otherwise, we won't televise.' The following year there was chaos.

✳ ✳

EXPENSE

Riding for children is a most inexpensive amusement, and a child can learn to ride very cheaply because the pony can be kept out at grass instead of in the stable. Thus kept, he will cost about 3s. a week, as against about 30s. for a stabled pony.

We must not, however, grudge money spent either on good lessons or good ponies; when our children have more good lessons, more money spent on their ponies, and more ponies kept out instead of in, we shall see a great improvement in riding. There will be many more happy riders, and the Golden Age for children and their ponies will have arrived.

The Young Riders Picture Book, 1936

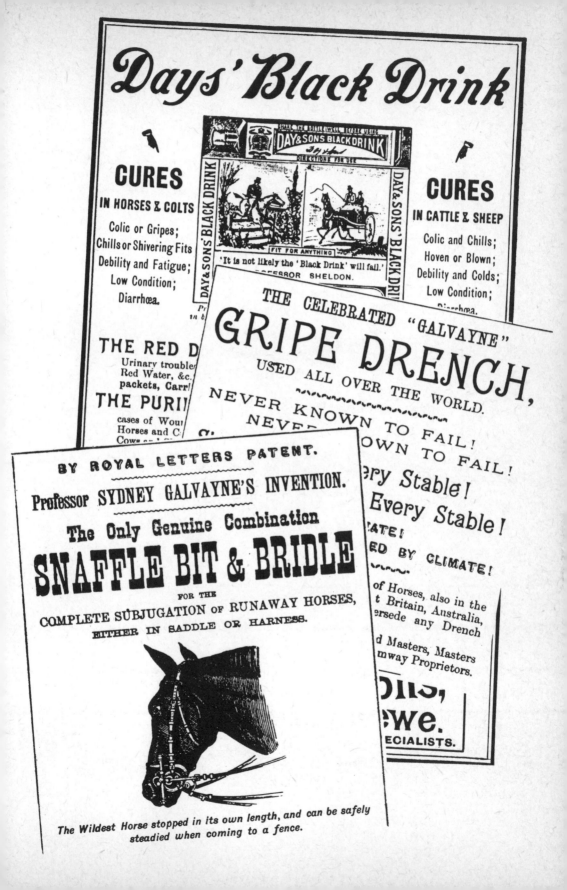

FIG. 178.—*Chaussure exploratrice* for registering the gaits by electricity.

PP', pedal with spring.
V, axis of the latter, unscrewing for cleaning.
G, frame for the pedal.
EE', screws fixing it to the shoe.

F, parietes of pedal forming a box.
C, one of the points of contact.
BB', knobs for attaching the conducting wires.
M, India-rubber membrane.

177.—Registering apparatus of Marey applied upon the horse at the trot.

FORE-RUNNERS OF FUTURE STYLES

The 'Clarissa'

The 'Mark'

The 'Richard'

Every picture tells a story

The up-market version of 'how many people can you get into a mini'

Eventing people do make provision for 'outsiders' at major events:
One door for gents – the tradesmen's entrance for men.

With attendance at major horse shows dropping over the past few years, the organisers have been struggling to find novel ways to attract the crowds back.

Every picture tells a story

Testing the brakes on the new Ford Mustang.

Horses and People

It's All Been Said Before

Xenophon, writing around 365 BC: 'As there will, doubtless, be times when the horse will need to race down hill and up hill and on sloping ground; times, also, when he will need to leap across an obstacle, or take a flying leap from off a bank, or jump down from a height, the rider must teach and train himself and his horse to meet all emergencies. In this way the two will have a chance of saving each other!'

Plus Ca Change

Sir Walter Scott (in *Rob Roy*): 'I believe there are few young men, and those very sturdy moralists, who would not rather be taxed with some moral peccadillos than with want of knowledge in horsemanship.'

Young Blade

The legendary Colonel 'Babe' Moseley (ex-Badminton co-director, team selector, steeplechase jockey), wanted to buy a new lawn mower. He therefore summoned half a dozen sales representatives to his garden, along with their machines, lined them up and gave them their orders. 'When I say "Go", start your mowers. The first one to the end of the lawn gets the order.'

French Letters

On her way to winning a European Championship with Cornishman V at Haras du Pin in France, Mary Gordon-Watson got lost on the Roads and Tracks. Frantically she hailed a passer-by, who was – like any Frenchman – pleased to chat to a young lady. Unfortunately, the best French Mary could muster was 'Fuzz Ah? Fuzz Say?', and her equestrian English was equally incomprehensible to the bemused man. But her desperate series of gesticulations conveyed her plight, and he did eventually point her back in the right direction.

Sauerkraut

Lucinda (Prior-Palmer) Green went for a fortnight to Germany, with her horse, for some combined enlightenment. Unfortunately the trainer had boils on his bottom, and could not ride for ten days.

Silly Ass

Moustached Colonel Bill Lithgow, former chef d'equipe and ex-chairman of the senior selectors, told his team they were not to take part in a donkey race during the 1974 World Three-Day Event Championships at Burghley. He ignored his own good advice, however, fell off the donkey, broke his ribs and had to run his team for the remainder of the event from his bed in the George hotel.

Tense, Nervous Headaches?

Richard Meade was ready to make his entrance in the 1976 Montreal Olympics, when he called to the girl helping him: 'Bonnie! My gloves! My stick! Where are they?'

'You've got your gloves on, and you're holding your stick.'

Sang froid was restored, and the Meade we all know was the one viewers throughout the world saw on their television sets.

To Bee Or Not To Bee?

Mary Gordon-Watson has felt the pressure of foreign ways. Continental bees are like huge hornets, and one positioned itself directly beneath her as she sat down to relax before starting on phase A at the Munich Olympics. Despite having to go through two hours in the saddle with a pulsating swelling on her bottom, she earned a gold medal.

Natural Selection

Lord Hugh Russell is a modest man, and chairman of the selectors from 1973 to 1976 – a period when the British team had very little success and a lot of bad luck. Discussing the difference between his style and that of his predecessor, he claimed: 'In the four years Martin (Whiteley) ran the team, they won everything. I felt I ought to do something different, so under me they won absolutely nothing.'

The Little Black Book

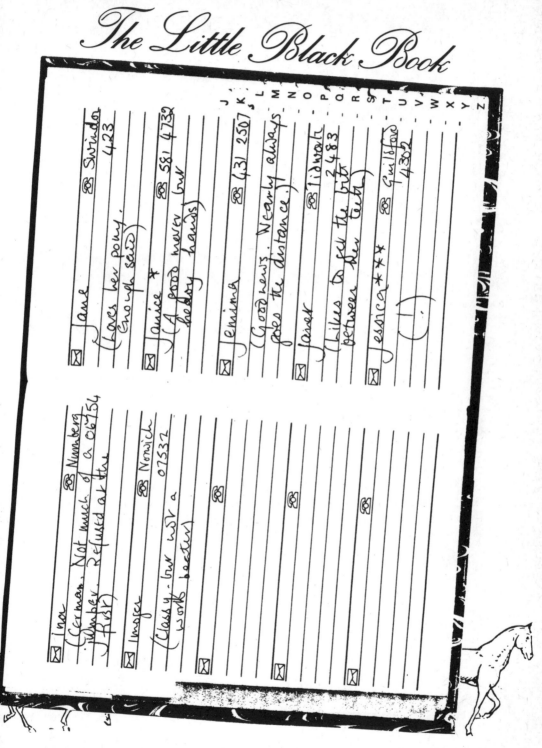

Spend a day in the grounds of a fairytale castle.

Join a five-mile queue of traffic and argue about who left the corkscrew at home. Get your car directed to the 'Range Rover park', miles from the action.

Tie your retriever to the bumper, unfold the tartan rug and set about the gin. Look the part in the Herbert Johnson cap or Hermès headscarf, and set off for a family day of fun.

Test your sense of direction – 'You are now in the "Volvo Car Park" – cross here'. Visit the trade stands to the north of the 'B.M.W. park', and buy anything from the Crown Jewels to whoopee cushions. Decipher the scoreboards, thrill at the garbled announcements about competitors spinning individually round a racecourse in the coach park.

Dedicated drinkers and terrier breeders can make use of our four-day package, staying in the luxury caravan park filling themselves with bacon sandwiches and Harveys Bristol Cream. Spend two days watching indifferent dressage tests, pass expert comment and let your dogs foul the cross-country fences (out of bounds for most of Saturday).

Spot the clones – the old tweedies who've been around longer than the house; the pairs of pony-breeding ladies in pork pie hats and brogue shoes; the army types, the 'hunter' booted country numbers, the Golf-driving young London set in their Knightsbridge punk outfits, and also the dedicated non-horsey hot-dog munchers and royalty-spotters. For fresh-air freaks there is an optional country ramble of four and a half miles (along with 200,000 others) taking in the occasional glimpse of a horse flashing past or crunching into solid timber. They only come past about every 20 minutes or so – they needn't spoil your enjoyment of forgetting where you've left the car or the children. Enjoy another traffic jam as you leave for home or stay for the thrilling climax on Sunday as the remaining competitors scatter beautifully-coloured poles round the arena and the band plays "Tie a yellow ribbon" . . .

Game for under fives

Re-arrange these shapes and design the Olympic Equestrian logo. It doesn't look much more like a horse and rider than drawing 1 does it?

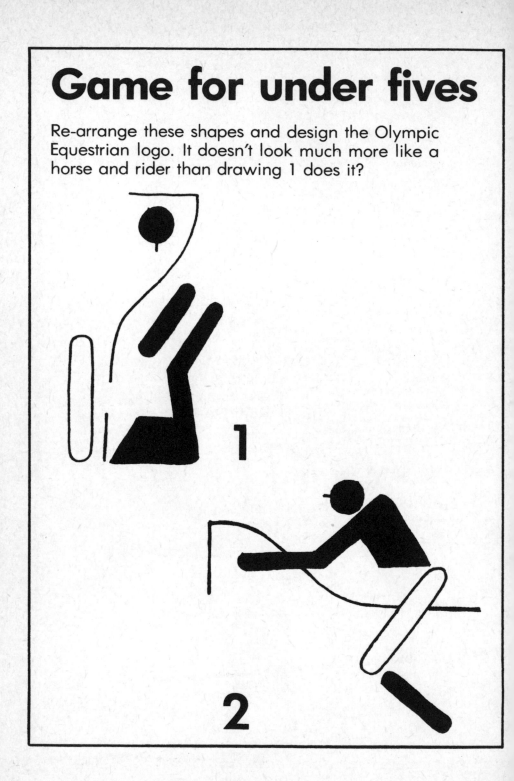

"NORTH RIDING," THE NOTORIOUS VICIOUS RACE HORSE.

"Professor GALVAYNE, however, with wonderful patience, subjected the horse to his treatment, which is a splendid exhibition of humanity and science combined, and at last was rewarded by getting the animal under control, so that he refused to kick under any circumstances."— *Sunderland Echo.*

"LORD LYON," THE VICIOUS CLYDESDALE STALLION.

"Lord Lyon is a particularly dangerous brute. He had one eye shot out by his owner to get him off a man he was worrying. At the termination of his second lesson Mr. GALVAYNE had him perfectly obedient to voice and whip—a most remarkable victory of man over the brute creation."—*Kilmarnock Herald.*

Fig. 16b.

"The sentences I heard Mr. GALVAYNE utter are so good that they ought to be written on the walls of every stable in the land. Here they are—'Vicious Men make Vicious Horses,' and 'A man should learn to govern himself before he undertakes to govern his horse.'"— *Newcastle Weekly Chronicle.*

"The animal handled was a biter, striker, and kicker, the property of N. Clark, Esq., of Beamish Park. *Note.*—She is now driven daily in Mr. GALVAYNE'S buggy, having been presented to him by the owner."— *Newcastle Journal, 14th Dec.*

VICIOUS HORSE BEING "GALVAYNED."

THE FIRST LEAP.

From the picture by Sir EDWIN LANDSEER, R.A.

114

Naughty Page!

Lower leg positions.

F.E.I. 3 DAY EVENT DRESSAGE TEST 1975

(unauthorised version)

1 A	Enter in 3rd gear, fixed grin, slam on brakes without changing down at	10
X	If female, drop one hand and peer down cleavage, if male remove hat in style of Fred Astaire about to descend 430 steps on lavish film set. Look up or replace hat respectively and proceed in second gear, ignoring first.	10
2 C	Hang left	10
S EBE	More juice, but slip the clutch slightly (JeeBy) large circle left, usually sort of egg-shaped but the judges can't see.	10
EV	Medium rare, with french fries please.	
3 V	Working overtime to remember the next bit.	10
A	Oh yes, up the middle along the neatly mown bit.	10
L	Follow Pooh and Piglet's Heffalump tracks to the left.	10
4 LS	Fail to find them after one circuit so crab to the left.	10
5 C	Lame and Halt – rain again – 'ere back off, John, ok, move along there please.	10

6 R
7 BEB
  BP
8 P
  A
9 L
  LR
	Do the whole lot again, only back to front	10

C	Stop – take the opportunity to start breathing again	10
10 HXF	Chance to be flashy and score maximum bonus as you extend merrily across the diagonal, triple axel and toe loops not required. Metallic nail varnish on hooves can add a bit of sparkle to this movement but remember to start applying brakes early	10
11 F	Regain control before KXM launching off across the other diagonal	
M	Slow down baby	

12 C	"Walkies"	10
HSXPF	Kink across the centre, don't rush this movement – you should be able to suck a whole Murraymint before reaching F	10
F	Keep going	
13 A	Canter round in a ridiculously tight circle	10
14 AC(DC)	Wiggle up the arena in 3 loops, the first and third, no problem, the second, tricky number this	10
15 MXK	Varooommm, screech . . .	10
16 K A 17 AC 18 HXF F	13–15 again, yes, back to front	10
19 A L	Up the mown bit again, awkward gear change	10
20 G	Finito. Time for a really overdone salute, winking and blowing kisses to the judges	10
	Let it all hang out TOTAL	200

Collective Marks:

1 Riders love life (freedom and regularity)	10
2 Riders love life (desire to move forward and backwards, elasticity of the hind quarters)	10
3 Submission (attention and obedience, freedom of movement and acceptance of a bit)	10
4 Positions and correct use of the aids (spurs, sprays etc, but whips not allowed)	10
MAX. MARKS	240

Fig. 18.   Fig. 18a.   Fig. 18b.   Fig. 18c.

What they say . . .

What they say . . .	And what they mean . . .
Your horse looks well	*It's fat*
Your horse looks very fit . . .	*Run up, thin*
(To a fellow competitor) That looked a nice careful round	*Why were you going so slowly?*
Good luck	*Don't hurt yourself, but don't do as well as me*
He felt a bit unlevel after the chase	*He was hopping lame but seems to be OK now*
I don't think jumping corners saves time	*I wouldn't jump them anyway*
He went beautifully, we just had this little bit of trouble	*I cocked it up*
It's nice to have that phase over with	*For god's sake someone get me a drink*
He's a super horse, he's just taking a long time to mature	*I've wasted five years and thousands on a dud and can't afford anything else now*
(To owner) I wonder if you could very kindly go and watch fence 25 for me	*For God's sake go away*
S**t I've fallen	*S**t I've fallen*
Typical horse trial weather .	*It's raining again*
That's a lovely new horse . . .	*How much did you pay for it?*
(From the selectors) That's a nice horse you've got	*Will you let someone else ride it?*

"Col. Mark Phillips on Rebozo the Second."
The loudspeaker interrupted her thoughts and her heart fluttered at the sound of his name.

A small murmur ran through the crowd, and suddenly she could see Mark, upright and noble, his spuggles glinting in the afternoon sunshine. Happy Rebozo! she thought to be so close to the man she loved.

And then he was off! He took the first fence in his stride and cantered down to the Three Bar Gate. Up and over! With Mark scarcely touching him with his jagger-whip, Rebozo vaulted majestically over the gate. Then 'The Short One', where so many lesser riders had caught thoir shockles on the horizontal yangling posts.

He was over! A ripple of applause greeted Mark. Anne found herself tightly clutching her fodder-cap, her first-ever present from this man on a Pegasus.

Only five hobblings to Bracey's Gap! Mark came thundering round Morley's Bend, his wenlock billowing behind him in the breeze.

God speed! Anne dared only whisper, for she felt all around her the prying eyes of the newspaper reporters that had for months now become like a black shadow to her and Mark, following their every move, exposing her deepest emotions to their crude and cynical gaze.

Mark took the jump with ease. Rebozo had wings, it seemed to Anne. But now it was the biggest test of all in the Seifert Cup – Rossiter's Ditch, three square runes of deep, cold water.

Anne held her breath and closed her eyes. His time was "well up". If he cleared this now the cup would be his. What a proud moment for both of them, should he win!

WHAT'S WHAT

BRITISH EQUESTRIAN PROMOTIONS – A company linked to the B.E.F. (see next entry) run by television mogul Raymond Brooks-Ward. It is responsible for finding sponsorship and money for equestrian activities.

B.H.S. – British Horse Society, based at Stoneleigh in Warwickshire at the National Equestrian Centre which it shares with the British Show Jumping Association – under the title the B.E.F. – the British Equestrian Federation. The B.H.S. oversees the national running of eventing, dressage, horse welfare and examinations.

F.E.I. – Fédération Equestre International. The international governing body of eventing, show-jumping, dressage and event driving. Prince Philip is President at time of writing.

THE HORSE TRIALS GROUP – A subsection of the B.H.S. which runs eventing in this country, from organising the fixture lists, to providing unpaid, appointed stewards to oversee individual competitions.

Glossary

Badminton Three-Day Event: a fair, notable for doggy beds and hamburgers. Those attending are sometimes inconvenienced by people on horseback.

Burghley Three-Day Event: as above, though on different site.

Coffin: cross-country jump (post and rails, ditch, post and rails). Also what unfit rider does after too many fags.

Dressage: part of three-day event in which competitors always do worse than they'd hoped, but never as badly as the judges think.

Drop fence: Instruction shouted by rider approaching over-sized obstacle.

Enter, down the centre line: see Serpentine

Extended trot: Prolonged bout of food poisoning (see **Badminton**, above, with special reference to hamburgers).

Flying change: Dressing ability required to ride more than one horse at a one-day event.

Hackamore: Othello's horsey brother.

Interrogator: either pleasant steward compiling provisional scores, *or* one's connections asking why one buggered it up.

Junior (and young riders) competitions: now affairs in which ready-made horses are ridden by offspring of self-made men.

Overfaced: term used in physical description of many riders.

Pelham: what many riders have in their mouths while talking.

Ping: term used by the excessively horsey of an athletic leap over a jump.
also sound made by overstrained elastic as they do so.

Pommell: effect on naughty bits when landed on.

Pony club camp: A grope activity.

Rein back: Canute-like order to attempt the impossible.

Ringworm: competitors' term for child who stands outside collecting ring asking for other people's autographs.

Serpentine: series of straight lines, linked by sharp corners. Similar to 'tacking' of yacht.

Snaffle: what girl riders do when they've made a pig's ear of it.

Splint: short, fast Chinese race.

Taxis: brush fence copied from the Pardubici steeplechase. Also what company-owned event horses can be written off against.

Upper Trout Hatchery: where many an eventer's mother originates.

Wonderful paces: rider's connections waiting in box at end of phase C.

Yorkshire boots: tie-on felt boots for horse's back legs, or hobnailed for riders walking course.

Idiomatic phrases
'Going a little deep': generally means totally submerged in the lake.
'That horse is really working through from behind': he did the worst dressage, but went well cross country.
'My horse developed a leg': not to be confused with 'He found a fifth leg at that fence'.

CAPTAIN WALKER (ENNISKILLEN DRAGOON GUARDS).
AS A RESULT OF CORRECT TRAINING AND IN SPITE OF EXTRAORDINARY CONFORMATION THIS HORSE WON MANY HORSE SHOW JUMPING COMPETITIONS AND WAS SECOND AT THE OLYMPIA INTERNATIONAL SHOW.

123

Every picture tells a story

'A child of ten or twelve who can look after his pony and go off alone for a ride cannot have much wrong with him, he is likely to be an efficient and valuable member of society later on.'
(The Young Rider's Picture Book, 1936)